Paper Elephants

Dedicated to all the fiery misfits

Contents

Forgotten

We start as hope
and end up as stories told
But to live and die
as forgotten art and unread poetry
is the biggest sorrow of them all

Beast

Love never was, nor will be, without chains
It demands a piece of your very core
An offering sought, forevermore
To give or not to give,
a fated sadness, either way
Nobody wins this battle
except for the beast in chains

Discriminate

Grief's a bastard
Terrorist's family or soldier's
It plays the same game
Pain treats all hearts' true
It doesn't discriminate, we do
We are the ones who choose
When and where empathy is due

Your eyes

Please don't blink
I see my world in your eyes, I plea
When your eyelids meet, alas
a fleeting blindness, I weep
Yet, I held onto hope within my heart's keep
that within the pause of a heartbeat
you'd reopen them again for me
Now I wander, bereft of sight
bumping into tragedies left and right
And asking you not to blink
is the worst thing I did
until the next thing I do
Open them for me once more, please

Shadow dweller

They say,
treat people the way you want to be treated.
But for some of us, in the shadows
it is an opportunity, a mirror,
a person with bones and blood like ours
Painting that pain onto another's skin
far simpler, far easier
So maybe, fellow shadow dweller
this time around, we learn
how we treat is not about us

Punctured

I live with a gaping hole in my chest
it never fully closes
I barely notice the blood
dripping into my cereal bowl
red shirts, red sheets
no sleep, no stitches
But then there came this soul
with their clean white shirt,
so bright, so pure
I stood close enough for our shadows to kiss
But when they opened their arms, I ran away,
my punctured heart, unprepared

Loud

I swim through the radio static
of thoughts overlapping
of screams and whispers
multitudes living in my brain
on top of each other
I can't see
I can't hear
It's too loud
It's too loud

Promise

I promise to be the last 1 percent in your battery,
the breeze that lets you know autumn is near
I will be the first ray of sun
after the winter that would never end
That t-shirt you thought you had lost forever
I promise, my dear, to be the rain in your desert,
the scrunchie on your wrist,
the first sip of your favorite whiskey,
and the hangover cure

Spectacular

I think of raindrops as little kisses
The sky turning pink is them blushing
I flirt with the moon
and they flirt back
I sing with the forests
and discuss existentialism with my plants
like my mother
and her mother,
this spectacular joy
of romantic femininity

Glorious trouble

They wished to be the peace
they thought I longed for
to be my happy ending, my quiet
Turns out I wasn't looking for them
I was looking for trouble instead
dying a little since 1998
nothing can break me
nothing can save me
So go save yourselves
and when you run, don't look back
cause I'll be running too
chasing glorious trouble
with a face like mine
a wicked smirk
a running high

Polaroid

You rode in on your motorcycle
at 5 in the morning
promising me sunrise on a beach
In the biting cold, through oversized jackets
I hugged you tight
Yet all that remains
of our expired love story
is a single Polaroid picture
captured by the sweetest old man
In this memory, frozen in time
we are kids with stupid grins
and sand between our toes
But behind the picture, I still see
the old man looking at us,
holding a secret, I'm sure
of another story, secretly alive

Tragedy

Tragedy fell in love with me,
comes to visit me
At first, I tried to escape her
But she is inevitable, insurmountable
So now I wait,
afraid that I might be falling as well
passionately, desperately
aching to feel something
the human condition,
the insanity of it all

Sky

You look like the sky
different cloud patterns, different colors
Somedays I even spot a rainbow
You stop me in my tracks,
every single time
And so, I'll spend my life reminding you
that you are worthy of stopping for a picture
of a pause

Moving day

Its moving day
cardboard boxes, the sound of tape
Packing my things, moving along
as I write this love letter
for a place, I didn't belong
Pink walls, white walls, grey walls, brick walls
all closed in, so I must go
to new neighbors,
and same polite hellos
I don't know how many square feet
I have loved them all
every set of keys
with every move, an extra box to seal
But this time, a secret wish
for a home, for two hearts, both belong,
beating together on a perfect night
"Don't go. Stay, please.
It might just feel right, my sweet"

Fun

Dancing in the rain is fun
Drying our hair, getting toasty in our pjs
and making hot chocolate is fun
Uncomfortably dripping wet on the doorway
and your cute little sneeze is fun
Not going out at all is fun
Accidentally stepping into another dimension
and fighting an army of bad magical dudes is fun
Maybe we have different commitments for the day
And I only see you for a minute
then muttering our I love yous
and falling asleep tired is fun
Maybe we fight, it'll be fun
Maybe we catch a flu
drinking hot tea and popping advils is fun
This day could go a million different ways
and I cannot imagine a single scenario
where I don't find fun in loving you

Stop speaking

In a dive bar,
sipping whiskey,
scribbling poetry on a cocktail napkin,
and these idiots won't leave me alone
No, I said.
my voice overthrown,
they kept speaking
No, I said
Towering over me,
the smell of cheap cigarettes
and their mum's basement,
their words kept coming
An insult to language
to silence, to me, to whiskey
And then came the hands
I drove a steel fork through my poetry,
a dent atop the wooden table, a good start
My knuckles, your teeth
let's step outside, measure our worth
Tallest in the room
with my stupid five-foot pride
I said No.
you should stop speaking.

Hi

Living endlessly in the moment we first said Hi

Vacant

I was, but a silhouette
a vacant body
Now with you,
in this feeling, I choose to stay
until it fills me up a little
day by day

Chai

My best friend woke me up at 6 in the morning
asked me if I wanted to go out for Chai
rubbing my eyes, I mumbled yeah let's go,
in last night's pajamas and unkempt hair
It started to rain
no umbrellas, but we didn't care
Wet hair stuck to our real faces,
we played football in a puddle
And when I finally got that hot cup of chai
it smelled like the first rain and joy
with a dash of cardamom
It smelled like my mom
A cigarette burned away on my left hand,
I forgot to smoke
as I drank my Chai
and looked at this beautiful morning I would've missed
if I had said No

Hurt

I want it to hurt
for me and for you
the terrifying happiness of being with you
the hurt that keeps me alive, away from you
tear-soaked pillowcases
on these silent lonely nights
I don't want to be alone
I want it to hurt
for me and for you

Dreamer

Madmen hate
cause they are taught not to see
The clever and creative sigh,
they see too much, they cry.
Meanwhile, there are dreamers,
people that look up at the sky
after the storm has passed
Praying to God.
knowing no answer will come by
Loving, knowing it will hurt
Dancing without limbs,
their happy tears, wild and free
for a tomorrow, they haven't yet seen.

Raincoats

Raincoat harms more than rain
In these fluent silences,
we found our way
But I think I'm ready now
to yell like a mad woman
to love like a mad woman
So, rip this raincoat off me darling
and let's fight in the rain

The storm

There is a storm raging beneath my skin
It would flood the earth if I let it
The weight pulls me closer to the ground
yet hurls me far, to the heavens
With careful labored steps, I bind it to me
until I can find my desert and be free

Hell

Hell is listening to the pitter-patter of rain
without ever knowing what it feels like on your skin
It is holding your favorite book
and not being able to smell it
It is listening to the sound of waves
crashing on the beach
and having no idea what it'll look like
when the sun goes down
It's knowing what you want
and not being able to touch it
It's loving someone you will never meet
It's incomplete
Hell is the feeling of incomplete.

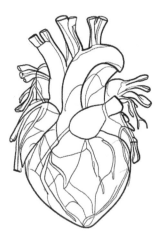

Shrunk

Let sorrow be kinder than man
For I'm afraid my heart's shrunk now that I am older

Shoes

"Walk a mile in somebody's shoes", they said,
"But what if they don't have shoes to wear?",
I thought in my head.
I never felt soil on my bare feet
Thorns and blisters
a pain imagined, incomplete
I own plenty of shoes, it's true
But even on the same road as you,
understanding, I could never pursue
Maybe I don't need to
perhaps we'll create a new shoe together
perhaps I'll take mine off and give them to you
So, tell me about that mile, that gravelly path
I'll listen to you
I'll come with, next time
Because my soft feet and your bruised one
would bleed the same color
that much, I know to be true
But if by chance, my friend,
you bled green, pink, or blue,
know that I'm still finishing that mile with you

When I knew

We were sitting on the balcony floor
your brown eyes with a hint of gold
You looked at me with the biggest smile
And for the first time in my life,
inside my head, it was quiet
Never in my wildest dreams
had I imagined peace
to be so extraordinary
That's when I knew
that a part of me will always belong to you

Maybe Suzy Maybe Juliet

Belonging to no country and no man
let's take our van
and chase this sunset
Maybe I'll be Suzy today, maybe Juliet
When vintage cameras
and old leather journals call
let's leave it all, run, fly,
and hopefully, even fall.

Words

Our lives are strung together
by a series of words that would never come
I hope you get to hear them
I hope you get to say them

Which face

We are a little bit of every face we've met
Did we learn to laugh
by watching or laughing
Did we learn to give
by watching or giving
Which face of mine would you like to meet first
The face of my lover I got bored of
or the face of my enemy I grew to admire
the dance moves I copied
the handshakes, the hugs or the knockout punches
All different faces, different times
I forget, how do people kiss again
Will you show me
You can choose any of your faces
I like your collection
Do you like mine

Wings

I secretly dream of wings erupting from my back
They are there
I feel them, itching to unfurl
So, I jumped out my window
Maybe I wanted to die a little
Maybe I wanted to fly a lot

Colors

Sitting on my father's shoulders
as he walked towards the ocean
Magically waking up in bed
after falling asleep in my mother's arms
Running and falling and running again
Hopes and dreams so far away
Maybe I'd be a firefighter
Maybe a movie star
My life, a gorgeous blank canvas
Now I can almost touch it, my someday
But rent bills food stands in the way
The colors are a little off every day
washed away from my canvas
again, and again and again

Twin birds

Once upon a time, there lived twin birds
One dreamt of a nest
and the other dreamt of the sun
But with wings stuck together,
they made home mid-air
A boundless, short, daring affair
Towards the dirt, together they dived
slowly, enough to fit a lifetime
And they fell, and they fell
Had they known the end was drawing near,
what words would they whisper
maybe hugged a little tighter, a little longer
Would they have ever let go
to feel the wind on their separated bodies
So, they stayed stuck, for their home
Plunging to their fate, they broke their gaze
Briefly to the earth, then to the sky
Their eyes met again,
wings unfurled, the earth quivered
For broken wings would hurt so much more
than a love that's free like never before.

Not mine

I was a liar to you
You were a liar to me
Maybe the antonym of a lie
is not the truth
Maybe, simply,
It was not my truth
What if we exist
in a space with
shared and infinite
parallel truths

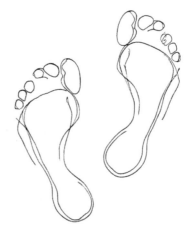

Footprint

I never told you I loved you
I hope to God you knew
So now I tell it to
the mailmen, the cashiers, the officers,
strangers, friends, and enemies
I can't stop saying it
because I'm here and you are not.
maybe I'm saying it for both of us
maybe I'm living for both of us
I gotta write a book,
Travel, learn how to cook,
I gotta sing and dance
make an impact, big and bright
to leave a footprint the size of two
Why am I here,
Why was I spared
I have everything to prove
to whom, I do not know
What I know, unfortunately,
is that I'm here and you are not
And no amount of I love yous now
can make up for the fact
that I never told you

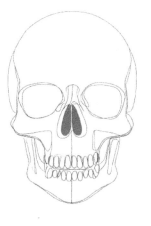

Skeletons

Skeletons,
echoes of what sets us apart
Worms crawl out of nameless skulls
from marked and unmarked graves
But If I plant an orange tree
above the ground, something just mine
Maybe I'll live forever
in this selfish legacy

Still

How fortunate are those who can sit still,
let their shoulders drop,
Watch that sunset without moving a muscle,
not take that picture, not move
watch the stars twinkle and leaves fall,
listen to birds singing and follow an ant or two,
perfectly still

The cost

"Loving me will cost you.", she said
"I'm a rich man.", he declared
"It'll cost you one mind.", she teased
"I am clearly not that smart, take it.",
he grinned, quite pleased
"It'll cost you one heart.",
she quipped, a twinkle in her gaze
"You already have it.", he chuckled, love ablaze
"It'll cost you one soul.", she dared with a wicked grin
"Whatever's left is yours, my dear, ask me more.",
he whispered, drawing in.

Story

Chasing a story
is always worth the trouble it brings
How dangerously delightful
to relish every second of it,
miss it and be hungry for more

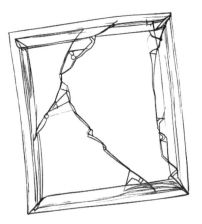

Bearable

I see you,
settling for bearable misery
How are you? I ask
Fine, you say
Always just fine
Smiles that don't reach your eyes
Your perfect picture
in this crooked frame
Why do you do this?
What's so bad about being lonely?
Do I make it look that bad?

All-knowing

Damn you
It's because of you
that I see it everywhere now
I see it in airports and hospitals
One look at the strangers in that cafe and I knew
It's because of you
The sweet sweet torture of knowing
and yet I couldn't be farther away
Is this maybe how God feels?
Alone and all-knowing
Is it really better to have loved and lost?
To be near only in restaged memories

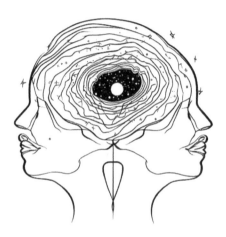

One person

We are one person
experiencing life subjectively
limb by limb, cell by cell
one organism, in infinite lifetimes
My laugh will echo
in the squirrels playing outside
My pain will reverberate
in my neighbor's cactus
and rock formations
But baby, our pain, our love is felt in the stars
Let me bask in your infinite glimmer,
your core memories, your grief
Let me into one of your universes
Let's just be, somewhere, everywhere, together
Let's feel the ground move beneath us,
because of us

The lion

Within me lives a lion bold,
with hunger, pride, and rage untold.
In the still of night, we chat like friends
He's terrifying, I'm told.
He loves me, this lion fierce and grand,
His roar shakes the earth, the land.
So, in a hidden cave, he fades away
This stunning lion that's part of me
Alone at his funeral,
under the sun, we shall meet

A little song

I am the little song you hum
when you are completely alone
I won't tell you my name
But know that we are by design
meant to carve out a little universe
a little calm, just ours
for this time being

Plant killer

Killed my plants today
Too much water, it seems
Bargained with God
"Please, oh please", with tears in my eyes,
"I'll offer you flowers.", said I
"I made them bloom, I have no need from you.",
said she
So, I stood there, in a graveyard of leaves
Tired and alone with stems that have sighed
until she tapped me on my shoulders,
and whispered into the wind
Love gives and love kills
it's the way of life, kid.

Bored

When or if suffering ends,
will reality end with it
Could art be without a little pain
Could I write poems that won't make us cry
Could we be tragically bored
with suffocating complicity

Best hug

We hugged
It was our best one
Standing on his doorstep
I almost said something
My lips quivered,
But instead, I smiled a bit
"Goodbye", I finally let out a sigh
I almost said something
Now I'm cursed to wonder
what might have been,
now lost to history

You are not my sun

I see you rising and setting
like clockwork, you fool me
Yet, you are not my sun, my friend,
for far too long, coldness does extend.
I see you peeking
Leave me be, imposter
because I remember,
midsummer nights with my love,
the wildflowers we picked
and the dragonflies we chased
Melting ice cream upon our hands,
polaroid memories on radiant sands.
The summer we promised
that would last a lifetime or two
But oh trickster, I implore you now
tell me, is this warmth? I forget.
Surely, you're not mine
for within my heart, a blizzard maligns,
a tempest that threatens to outlast me
If you're my sun,
why am I so blue

The Devil and I

I escaped your heaven
to have a drink with the devil
This climate is red hot
and so am I
We roasted marshmallows over lava
and ridiculed fluffy tasteless clouds
Said nobody loves him
when he needs it the most
but I'd gladly burn the world down
to keep him warm

Wet sand

How funny it is that
the fear of not moving paralyzes you,
feet buried in wet sand,
down you go with every passing wave
You could've swam, you could've moved
Instead, you watch the sharks and the jellyfish
You watch the sea kidnapping you
You watch without movement,
sinking and thinking how funny it is

The one

Do you ever rank heartbreaks
There are the ones
you wouldn't wish on your worst enemy
There are the ones you'll never tell
And then there is the one that pulls you back
The one you wouldn't take back
The one you wish you could live again

Little lies

Memories are little lies
by us, for us
Pink skies, background music
That hug, a few seconds longer
That eye contact didn't last forever
Little lies
You didn't love me
I loved you loving me
Little lies

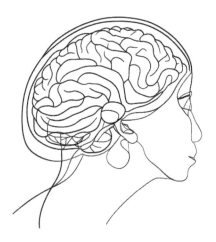

Arch-nemesis

My arch-nemesis and I
live together in my head
I wonder what'll happen
When we finally run out of space

Break in

Break into my heart
I'll leave it open for you.
Take down the walls and redecorate,
destroy it and mend it again,
We'll build a home
and take a hammer to it
Occupied, indefinitely
in this heart, is all versions of us

Thousand

Death by a thousand cuts
your thousand words
I bleed out on the floor
It's not the pain I dread
but knowing that
I'll see you tomorrow morning,
and the morning after
and the morning after that
Yet you will never run out of words
and I'll never run out of blood

Show me a God

Show me a God
that knows what it's like
to go to bed hungry
to kiss a stranger on a balcony overlooking Paris
to tuck your kids in at night
to be surprised
to stub your toe
to build a home
to be homeless
to be hopeless
to grieve
Show me anything other than rage and ego
cause you can't love if you can't feel
Show me this truth and I'll still stand tall
No bowing, no kneeling, no curtain call
Because I have loved, my dear
and it was godlier than God, beyond compare

Fear

I am afraid of many things
But mostly I'm afraid
of an empty waiting room
of the memory that'll play
when I close my eyes
the final certainty of regret

String

Feet above, never touching the ground
our home was a string
tied to big strong hearts
And apart, we broke with it
The string that once was
now a relic

What I am

What I see is what I am
What I feel is my map
To where, doesn't matter

This world

This world's a lot bigger than our love story
It still turned, and I, with it

Blood

Is dying without wounds
worse than living forever?
Why is my blood expensive?
Does it have glitter?

Ink

You live in the worn pages
of the book I enjoy re-reading
But by the time
my ink touches paper
it's gone
you are gone

Falling

I'm the last yellow leaf
on a ghostly tree in October
I must fall

The fool

Forgive me
it wasn't cool
I love big
And so, I play the fool
wired like this, for this
I don't know any other way

Heisenberg

Heisenberg showed us
a quantum decree,
Know your place or speed, not both, you see
Yet, I crave this paradox
to defy cosmic laws
to know it all,
and to have everything

Paper Elephants

Once smaller,
with a spine so bent,
I went on a quest
with tons on my chest
Through time, I chose to swim
To my surprise,
I didn't drown within
When I looked again,
I found Paper Elephants,
with stories to share
So now I float with them
Tall and light
in this free air

Acknowledgements

To my parents, Babu Eapen and Bincy Babu-
Your unconditional support has been my foundation.
Even in moments when I felt undeserving, you stood
by me, and for that, I am eternally grateful.

To my little brother, Sebin Babu Eapen(Appu)-
Your wisdom grounds me. I am in awe of the person
you've become, and I am fortunate to have you as
family.

To Lea Rouillier, my anam cara-
Your brilliant unwavering presence has made me a
better person. Thank you.

To all the people and places that inspired these poems-
Thank you for making this life pretty.

And to my readers-
You have changed the trajectory of my life. Your faith
in me and my works is nothing short of incredible.
Thank you for being a part of this journey and for
showing me how powerful words can be.